Fashion Designers and Fragrance

To: Allison

Dedication

To my Mom and Dad, Nannie L. and Harold Barnwell, to my sister Bonita and brother Harold Jr. and my nephew Jovan whom have shaped and continue to shape my life.

Fashion Designers and Fragrance

The Perfect Brand Extension

Andre' Barnwell

StE Saw the Elephant

First edition
Saw the Elephant Books

ISBN 978-0-692-43629-5 (pbk.)

Library of Congress Control Number: 2015907619

Table of Contents

Acknowledgments

This book is designed to spark your interest in fragrances and by no means should be the last book your read on the subject.

My purpose with this book is to demystify some of the language and techniques used in the fragrance business and to give you the fashion designer the tools needed to ensure success of your brand extension: a fragrance.

You are working so hard to expose your brand in the highly competitive fashion industry and at the same time your brand has the potential to be associated with a fragrance in a bottle. Your story could be expressed thru fragrance and your fragrance will be associated with you and your fashion brand forever.

Introduction

You never know where paths may lead in life and my story is no different. I didn't start out as a fragrance designer but as a tie designer. My entrance into the fashion world would be as I thought it would by designing men's ties. My marketing strategy was quite simple, create unique ties for myself to wear to work and self promote.

Let me go back into my past to give you some context. I grew up in Yeadon, Pa. a small town outside the city of Philadelphia. I decided to leave Pennsylvania for college and attended the University of Houston and subsequently transferred to Howard University in Washington, DC where I earned a business degree in Marketing. I stayed in the Washington, DC area after graduating from Howard and eventually landed a job at Xerox Corporation in Rosslyn, Virginia as a customer business representative. It is here in Virginia while working at Xerox where my fashion journey started.

I noticed immediately that the culture at Xerox was to dress well. Men wore suits in those days, double breasted suits and flashy, nice ties were common. I got to thinking that ties would be my entrance into the fashion world. Xerox I thought is exactly the place to showcase my ties. In addition, our "rival" in dress for men was IBM. However, IBM was known for singled breasted suits with conservative ties and Xerox was a little more fashion oriented with single and double breasted suits with more fashionable ties and accessories like cuff links, tie bars and pocket squares. With this as my motivation, I set off to become a tie designer. I had taken a sewing class in high school but nothing else (shout out to Yeadon High School, it no longer exists as a school but forever in my heart). I decided to make a dog out of corduroy material and my mom still has it at our house! Okay back to the story, I bought a tie pattern and the supporting materials and tools from a fabric store, borrowed my sister's sewing machine (thanks Sis!) set up a spot in my studio apartment and was ready to go! As a marketing major, I knew it was important to name my brand so I called it Cravates by Andre' Barnwell, "cravates" being French for tie. I dutifully and with discipline used my spare time to develop my sewing skills on my sister's machine. Mastering the use of a sewing machine is really hard at least it was for me and it gave me a deeper appreciation for the designers and seamstress workers that use them. I quickly realized that my creative interests had been sparked by my new path but I also realized I was gravitating more to the designing elements in general and not to those elements as they related to fashion. But one to not quit a new endeavor "too early", I kept creating ties with the hope that it would inspire other outlets to express my creativity.

One Saturday morning, I decided to go to the Martin Luther King Jr. Library in downtown Washington, D.C. to do some research on additional sources for sewing materials when my epiphany struck. About 45 minutes into my stay at the library, I just didn't feel like researching. I told myself that I wouldn't leave the library but would take a break in hopes that my enthusiasm for researching would come back. I decided to browse the reading and magazine section of the library and to my surprise I found a "How To" book on creating a fragrance and it hit me! That's it! Its not ties its creating a fragrance and not a fragrance for women but for men and I could use myself as the guinea pig. I knew this was it. I continued to read the book and from that day on I knew I was a fragrance designer. In a matter of days, I packed away all my sewing materials gave my sister back her sewing machine (thank you Bonnie) and started the process of ordering fragrance supplies so I could start making my own fragrance. I don't believe in luck per say, but I do believe in allowing new ideas to come to you and not being afraid to act on them.

I took the position of focusing on fragrance as a smell pleasure. Aromatherapy as a discipline explores smell from a healing perspective. If aromatherapy is your interest there are many good books on the subject. It is however not the area I wanted to pursue with my career.

The rest of the book is what I've learned over 20 years as a fragrance designer and over 16 years teaching fragrances and branding to high school and college students. It is this experience and knowledge I'd like to share with you. My goal is for you to use this book as a guide to developing your sense of smell and encourage you to include a fragrance in your product line to accompany your fashion brands.

Brand & Brand Extensions

Okay fashion designers what is going to be the most important decision you will have to make in your professional fashion career is how will you brand yourself? What will be the name of your fashion line? Will you name it after yourself, a combination of you and your partner in business or will you name it after a concept? Think names like Gucci, Chanel, Vera Wang, Micheal Kors, Ozwald Boeteng, Tom Ford, Calvin Klein, Tracy Reese, Tommy Hilfiger, and Betsey Johnson or in partnership like Dolce & Gabbana or lifestyle/concepts like True Religion, American Apparel, and Nike etc. According to the American Marketing Association (AMA), a brand is a "name, term, sign, symbol, design or combination of them intended to identify the goods and services of one seller or group of sellers and to differentiate them from those of competition."

Take your time in coming up with your brand name. Starting with your birth name which is probably the easiest to own as a trademark unless your name is also famous before you. Eventually add a symbol and then possibly a term. I always think what feels right for you and your customers; you'll know them better than anyone else. High end brands tend to use their names and possibly a logo, casual lines and sports apparel lines tend to use a non personal name, symbol and term (i.e. Nike, "The Swoosh", Just Do It).

The only good brand is one that you own. So let's look at the first steps you should take. The two places I go first are www.uspto.gov (United States Patent and Trademark Office) and www.godaddy.com (a domain company). There are other domain companies that you can select as well but Godaddy is the one that I use.

When you go to uspto.gov you are going to click on:

Trademarks then click
Searching Trademarks then click
Trademark Electronic Search System
Then click Basic Word Mark Search

Type in your name where you see "search term" to see if your brand name is already owned. You want to pay special attention to the last column Live/Dead. If it says Live then the word mark is actively owned by whoever registered it. If the column says Dead that word mark has expired and is available for registration to a new applicant. If you type in a name and "no tess records found" appears, this name was never applied for before. Others parts of the website will show step by step the application process you will need to register your brand. Even if you have someone to do this for you it is important for you to understand the process and more importantly the actual costs involved in registration of brands. Each classification you want the brand to be in has a separate fee. For example, the classification for fashion is 025 and the classification for fragrance is 003. If you want your clothing line and fragrance to be under one brand you would pay for each separately. You might be surprised what the government fee is and what lawyers or business consultants might charge you.

A registered trademark with the government allows you to use this mark ® next to your brand. You can only use this when the government acknowledges you are the owner of the brand thru official correspondence. It took me 3 years from the time I turned in my application in until I received my official documents that I owned RAKS. Today, with on-line processing this process could be done in a matter of days.

If you don't have the ® yet, you also might have noticed brands using a ™ symbol. This symbol can be used without official registration. Why use the ™? It is letting other people in the marketplace know that you are intending to use the brand name.

The other site that I go to is godaddy.com and type in the name to see if the URL (uniform resource locator) is available or taken. I typically go here first. If the URL is taken, the brand name is probably in the process of being trademarked as well.

The brand that we all have is our names and using them will get the customers to focus on you. Who you are and what your brand represents is the "heart and soul" of your brand. The term used to describe this is the brand mantra or also referred to as the brand essence. An easy way to create your own brand mantra/essence is by using the 3 word format: adjective, adjective, noun. Madonna's mantra/essence was audacious, sexual, chameleon a company like Nike was authentic, athletic, performance for example.

Once you establish your name in the marketplace, you should also consider including a symbol for your brand (that symbol when used on your product is called the logo). While the language of your name needs customers to understand it, symbols are universal and help in making your brand global, when you see Chanel' two C's logo, do you need to see the word Chanel?

If you're going to include a signature color or colors to your brand, it might be helpful for you to understand how people already react to certain colors from a psychological and/or emotional standpoint. There are many connections between colors and people and here are a few:

Blue - most calming
Red – conveys power and sexy
White – clean, fresh, cool
Yellow – cheerfulness
Black – elegance and sophistication
Purple and Gold – royalty

Once you select a color(s), it is very important that you reinforce its use with the brand. Think how powerful the color blue is with Tiffany & Co.

I have given you some of the ways you can get to the brand choice you want. But at the end of the day what you choose and why is your choice as a designer, you should be the final say. If there is a story behind why you choose this name or that name, this color or that color as long as you share that with your customers they will understand. You'll be surprised how much they appreciate your openness with them of your creative process.

An interesting story that I share with my students is how Michael Kors branded his fashion line. When you ask most people about Michael Kors's name most would say that his real name. However, it is not his real name. Michael was born Karl Anderson, Jr. When his mother remarried Bill Kors, she gave him his stepfather's last name Kors but his mother also allowed Carl to change his first name as well, and he decided on Michael David Kors.

Now that you have decided on your brand name for your clothing line, a fragrance would be considered a brand extension. A brand extension is used to enter a new market or market segment. There are two types of brand extensions (1) a line extension using your current brand to enter a new market segment in the existing product class for example you started with dresses and now your making blouses or (2) use your current brand to enter a different product class which is what this book is about taking your brand in fashion and extending it into the beauty business specifically the fragrance industry.

Try this branding exercise:

A. Think of your first name, middle name and last name in any combination that works for you.

1. Andre' Barnwell
2. A. Barnwell
3. Andre' B.
4. In my case I don't have a middle name. (only use two words, replace your middle name for either of your names)

B. Think of a logo for yourself.
(you could use your initials as your logo)

C. Which colors would you use and why?

D. Create your brand mantra using the 3 word format adjective, adjective, noun.

Why do I want you to play with different ways to use your name? From a business perspective, it is easier to register your name then made up names.

Ways to Extend Your Brand

When you're thinking about extending your brand from a business strategy perspective you have several options.

You could (1) go to a private label company that manufactures fragrances and purchase from them a fragrance and put your name on it. You typically have to select from a fragrance formula that they have already created, they will send you their samples upon your request and you select the one you like. That fragrance won't be exclusive to you but because your name is on it separates you from someone else who purchases it and uses another name. You just hope that your fragrance and their fragrance are not sold in the same place.

(2) A company can pay you for the rights to use your name on their fragrance. This is called licensing. For a fee, you are letting the company use you name on their product. This usually occurs when your brand name has exposure in the public arena where they see potential in future sales using your name on their product. Say you win a fashion reality competition or a fashion magazine wrote an article on you as a top up and coming designer or a celebrity wore your clothes and commented in the media of how they loved your clothing. A licensor would likely approach you based on this publicity in the media. Even though this is good you still have to make sure that licensing is right for you

because the licensor does own your name now in this category of fragrance for whatever the time frame you agreed to in your contract. So as far as controlling your brand this category of your brand name is controlled by the licensor and they will have the final say on marketing decisions for your fragrance. Things to consider before making a deal with them; make sure the fragrance strategy they use is not in conflict with your fashion line strategy. For example, if you have an upscale fashion line your fragrance line should also support this strategy.

(3) You could manufacture the product yourself and market it with your fashion line strategy as you see fit. You will have to then fund this project yourself and I would recommend hiring a fragrance designer to create the needed elements of smell, bottles, and packaging considerations for you to approve at the proper stages in the product development process. Remember, you are still working and devoting your time on the needs of your fashion line and you should consider not trying to do all of this by yourself. The ability to delegate aspects of your business to responsible people will be a successful tool for you beyond just a fragrance line.

You might be thinking why bother? The answer is a successful fragrance is a very lucrative business for you to be in. The profits from this brand extension could support parts of your fashion business. Off setting costs for runway shows, advertising, additional pieces to your fashion line and general expansion of your fashion business to name a few. Remember, your fragrance is now exposing your brand name in the beauty market which is a multi billion dollar industry. This might be the first place a potential customer has been exposed to your brand name and if they like your fragrance they will probably have a positive reaction to your fashion line. The top fragrances in the world are typically brand extensions of fashion lines.

Also, the outlets for your fragrance are usually broader than your fashion line. Beauty stores, drugstores, duty-free at airports, niche retail stores, general retail stores are all places where customers are comfortable buying fragrances including yours.

The World of Fragrances

Many civilizations have contributed to the development of the fragrance business as we know it today but here are some key ones you should know.

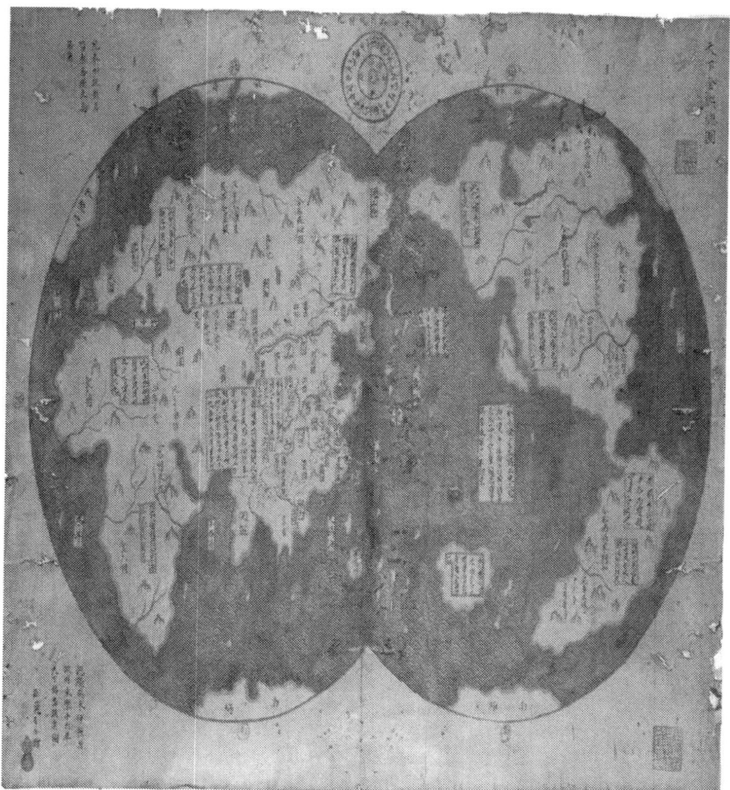

1763 Chinese Map of the World

Africa

Egyptian perfumers made cones and other scented products using the maceration process. The scented cones were placed on the top of a woman's wig and would slowly melt over time releasing its scent.

Cleopatra would anoint herself with rose scented oils especially her lips so when she kissed a man her scent would linger on him long after the kiss. The sails of her ship were perfumed as well.

Egyptians burned incense resins favorites were frankincense and myrrh which they got from Punt (which is believed to be Somalia and Northern Ethiopia).

Cleopatra; Michaelangelo Buonarroti (1475 – 1569)

East
(Far East, Middle East, Near East)

Islamic science allowed for the development of organic chemistry and the experimentation of distillation techniques.

Muslim traders connected cultures through the "spice" caravans (pepper, cloves, frankincense and myrrh resins, syrups flavored with roses and violets).

Persia (modern day Iran) had a culture that encouraged the lavish use of scented oils for both men and women.

Middle East Map, 1540

Asia

When Muslim traders reached China with their spices and scents, the Chinese became avid consumers of whatever fragrances were brought to their doors.

China made great improvements in distillation techniques. They introduced a step by which ethyl alcohol was extracted from wine.

Refinements of Chinese culture including fragrance were carried to the neighboring countries of Korea and Japan by monks and trade delegations.

Yu the Great, mythic founder Xia Dynasty

Europe

In the city states of Athens and Corinth (now Greece), they blended and exported oils perfumed with macerated rose, lily, iris, sage, thyme, marjoram, mint and anise.

The people of Rome loved rose oil the most of all. The famous baths of Rome were among the places where perfumed products were regularly used.

The English word perfume in Latin is *per fumme* meaning “thru smoke.” The French word for perfume is parfum.

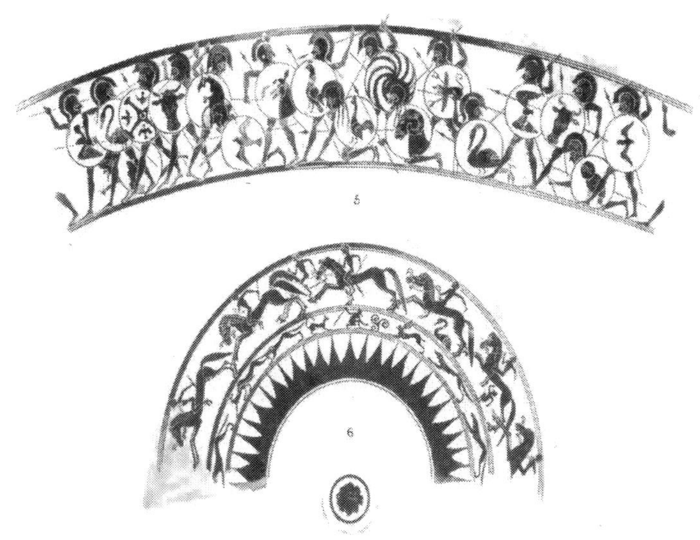

Greek perfume bottle design

Europe and the Modern Fragrance Industry

The distillation process was perfected in 1320 in Italy resulting in the use of an alcohol that was 95% alcohol.

The first "perfume" would occur 50 years later in 1370 called Hungary Water which was alcohol blended with rosemary and lavender and was allegedly named after Queen Elizabeth of Hungary.

Jicky by Guerlain was the first "modern" perfume, created in 1889; it was a synthetic mixture and its creative goal was to create a smell not found in nature.

Catherine De Medici
(1519 – 1589)
The Ambassador of Perfume

Catherine encouraged the development of the perfume industry in France. Catherine was Italian by birth but married King Henry II of France and lived long enough to see three of her son's become Kings of France (Francis II, Charles IX and Henry III).

Grasse, France became the center of the perfume industry during her lifetime.

Fashion Greats & Fragrances

"A perfume should express the spirit of the age, reflecting the aspirations and moods of it's time while remaining apart from changes in fashion."

- Christian Dior (1905 – 1957)

Paul Poiret
(1879 – 1944)

In 1911, Paul was the first to have the idea of marketing a perfume to compliment his line of clothing.

La Rose de Rosine was named after his oldest daughter and was created by Henri Alméras in 1911.

The most successful fragrances in the world are associated with fashion brands. However, the number of new fashion designers that should be on that list is lower with the emergence of non fashion designers like musical artists, actresses, actors and general celebrities using fragrance as a way to extend their brands. Remember just like your clothes, people "wear" fragrances and it is this natural connection that new fashion designers must reclaim.

Gabrielle Bonheur "Coco" Chanel

(1883 – 1971)

Coco in collaboration with perfumer Ernest Beaux, who was the first to employ "aldehydes" a powerful synthetic and the rest is history….Chanel No.5 (1921).

"A woman who doesn't wear perfume has no future."

- Coco Chanel

Jeanne Lanvin
(1867 – 1946)

"Perfume demanded an exceptional bottle and one which broke with the styles of time." – Jeanne Lanvin

Arpege was created by Paul Vacitee and Andre Fraysse in 1927.

Arpege was put in a bottle celebrating the style of a Grecian urn.

Portrait of Jeanne Lanvin

Jean Patou
(1880 – 1936)

"A sophisticated woman should avoid all eccentricity, in the choice of a perfume as much as in that of a dress, applying the same discreet sense of taste and elegance to her scent as to her wardrobe." – Jean Patou

Joy was created by Henri Alméras in 1930.

Top Fashion Designers in the Fragrance Business Are You The Next?

You'll notice that these well known top designers brand themselves using their personal names. Customers identify more with people than products especially in the fashion industry. There is a strong emotional connection between your name and your story. This could be a personal story of why you are a designer or it could be your philosophy you live by. So when they buy your fragrance there are in fact buying into your story. It is the goal of all successful brands to have an emotional connection to their customers.

The Perfumers & Jewelers

We owe a lot to the perfumers and jewelers whose passion for fragrance as an art has allowed exquisite fragrance formulas and bottle designs to give the fragrance industry "classic" status.

Ernest Beaux
(1881 – 1961)

Ernest was the first perfumer to employ aldehydes as a synthetic booster and created Chanel No.5 in 1921.

Why was it called Chanel No. 5? It has been said that Coco selected Ernest's number 5 formula and said, "I will call it Chanel No.5."

Other perfumers of note, Sophia Grojsman (Eternity, 1988), Calice Becker (Tommy Girl, 1996), Jacques Polge (Coco, 1984), Francis Kurkdjian (Armani Mania, 2002) and Maurice Roucel (Envy, 1997).

Francois Coty
(1874 – 1934)

Francois was the first to blend natural and artificially produced fragrances. He was obsessed with creating fragrances and presenting them in beautiful bottles.

To this day, many customers select their fragrances because of their bottle design. Many customers like to showcase their fragrances and bottle varieties create a better visual experience.

Top jewelers in the fragrance business like Van Cleef & Arpels, Cartier, Boucheron and Bulgari share in Francois's passion for the exquisite bottle.

Some Industry Definitions you should know

Olfactory fatigue – our sense of smell is arguably are most powerful but at the same time our weakest. Our sense of smell tires easily, so when we smell scents, we should smell no more than three at a time before resetting our nose.

Fragrance – the pleasantness of smell, remember perfume is just one type of fragrance.

Scent – a distinctive, often agreeable odor.

Anosmia – loss of our sense of smell. This could be temporarily when we have a cold or allergy that affects our sinuses or a permanent condition sometimes brought on by a head trauma in some kind of accident (car, motorcycle, bicycle etc...).

Aromatherapy – healing through aroma.

The Nose (perfume blender) – a person who creates fragrances.

Fragrance designer – creates fragrances, bottle selection and packaging.

Organ – structure that holds your fragrance materials usually in the shape of a musical organ.

Fixative – essential/fragrance oil used for the purpose of controlling the volatility of a fragrance.

Alcohol – denatured ethyl alcohol is added to a fragrance to facilitate burn off.

Cologne – is actually a town in Germany and it's usually used as a category for men's fragrance.

Pulse points – wherever the pulse of your heart beat is closest to the surface of your skin.

Natural spray – non-aerosol spray that has a mechanism that produces a mist spray.

Fragrance Geographical Facts

Grasse, France – historical capitol of the fragrance business known for its jasmine, rose and orange production.

Paris, France - first commercial capitol of the fragrance business.

New York City, USA - modern capitol of the fragrance business.

North Jersey, USA -synthetic fragrance capitol.

Rue de Rivoli, Paris, France, 1854.

Essential vs. Fragrance Oils

Natural oils come from organic i.e. live products like animals, plants, flowers, fruits etc. and are called "essential" oils. They are very expensive to produce and can vary in availability because of variations in the source product. For example, the scent of lemons grown in Italy smell different from lemons grown in California or Florida. The soil, climate and weather conditions all play into how something smells. Essential oils do however have distinct smells and are a favorite of those who can afford them.

Synthetic oils are chemical reproductions of essential oils and are called fragrance oils. Fragrance oils are man-made reproductions of the essential oils using synthetic and essential oils together. The majority of perfumes/colognes on the market are synthetic fragrances. For example, the essential oil of oranges comes from extracting the oil from the orange peel. The fragrance oil is the chemical formula of the orange oil created by recreating it with chemicals and done in a very economical way. The term aroma chemical is also used to describe these synthetic formulas.

The development of animal synthetics is for me the most important need for synthetics. It has allowed us to recreate essential oils derived from animals which in the past we would have had to destroy animals to collect.

Essential oils and fragrance oils are highly concentrated and have to be used with caution. They should not be applied directly to the skin without first being diluted with an alcohol or non-alcohol base.

Lastly, when purchasing oils, if it's called "oil of orange," it's an essential oil. If it's labeled "orange oil" it's a fragrance oil. (So if the word "oil of" precedes the ingredient it's an essential oil if the word "oil" is after the ingredient it's a synthetic oil (fragrance oil).

Fragrance Manufacturing Naturals

Rodolphe Ernst (1854-1932) “The Perfume Maker”

Expression

Fruits with skins rich in essential oils (citrus-lemon, lime, orange, grapefruit and bergamot).

Pressed to render oil.

Oldest and simplest method of deriving natural essences from plants.

Lily perfume making, 4th Dynasty of Egypt (2500s BC)

Ancient still for extraction of essential oils, 1897.

Distillation

Raw botanical mass in water and boiled.

Allowed extraction from a wide variety of plants.

Not good on citrus and flowers because of heat.

Allowed for the manufacture of alcohol at higher concentrations.

Enfleurage

Extracting essences from flowers.

Peddles are individually placed on top of butter/fat between glass plates. The butter/fat slowly extracts the oil from the flower petals over time.

The butter/fat oil is known as a pomade, you add alcohol to obtain the essential oil.

No heat is used so as to not damage the delicate flowers.

Enfleurage was eventually replaced by the technique solvent by extraction.

Enfleurage, A. Chirls Factory, Grasse, 1930.

Other Natural Manufacturing Processes

Solvent by Extraction

A liquid solvent (hexane) is circulated over the flowers to dissolve the essential oils.

A waxy paste called a concentrate is produced.

If the concentrate is mixed with alcohol the resulting oil is called an absolute.

Solvent by extraction replaced enfleurage.

Maceration

Similar to enfleurage but performed at higher temperatures.

Flowers and other plant parts are warmed in hot vegetable oils or animal fats.

Mixture is filtered and allowed to cool.

This process along with expression was used by the Egyptians.

If you like to see some of these natural manufacturing processes in a historical context, I recommend you watch the DreamWorks' movie Perfume: The Story of a Murderer released in 2006. It's about a man with an incredible sense of smell and his deadly quest for creating the perfect perfume.

The cinematography is excellent and the attention to detail when showing the natural manufacturing processes are well worth it. It is however rated R for subject matter.

Fragrance Families

The reason we organize scents into families is because it helps us organize in our minds the types of scents you like without having to smell all of them. You will soon thru smelling scents recognize the one's you like in general. If you prefer spicy, fruity and animal over other families, you will probably want a combination of them in your final formula.

Woody
freshly cut aromatic woods

Resinous
ducts in the bark of trees

Animal
derived from animals

Balsamic
vanilla or spicy overtones

Earthy
stale smell, turned soil

Green
fresh and leafy

Edible
associated with food

Mosses
damp, earthy

Light
airy quality

Spicy
savvy spicy notes

Citrus
light, fresh, tart

Narcotic
hypnotic and calming

Fruity
fruit & herbal

Precious
depth, harmony

Floral
from flowers

Fragrance Types

When you are ready to sell your product we don't use families but types. The types you use will be determined by the emphasis of your fragrance the dominant factors of the following types.

Floral

Single as well as bouquets of flowers
ex. L'Air du Temps

Floral/ Fruity

Newer category, blends of flower and fruity notes
ex. Lauren

Oriental

Warm, spicy, long lasting
ex. Opium

Aldehydic

Also known as "modern", aldehydes and synthetics combined
ex. Chanel No. 5

Chypre

Sophisticated earthy based on accords
Patchouli and oak moss are apart of all formulas
ex. Miss Dior

Fougere'

Herbaceous scents mainly male colognes
ex. Cool Water

Citrus

Fresh, crisp scents
ex. Armani

Green

Fresh natural "outdoors" scent
ex. Alfred Sung

Your fragrance types should reflect your personal preferences in scent. Remember people are buying into your story. Never select fragrance types just because they are popular but those that inspire you. I created a cologne with Fougere' types that I would wear or if I created a perfume it would be a scent that I would enjoy on a woman like Florals and Orientals'.

Fragrance Categories

The percentages are how we relate oil to the percentage of alcohol in the fragrance. i.e. 15 % oil plus 85% alcohol = 100%.

Fragrance names associated with ladies lines:

1. **Perfume or Parfum**
   15 to 30%
   (Perfume comes from the Latin meaning "through smoke." Perfume in French is Parfum)

2. **Parfum de Toilette/**
   Eau de Parfum (EDP)
   8 to 15%
   Eau de is French for "water of."
   (Important Note: Eau de Parfum and Perfume is not the same thing)

3. **Eau de Toilette**
   4 to 8%

4. **Eau de Cologne**
   3 to 5 %
   (Cologne name after the German town of Cologne)

5. **Splash Cologne**
   1 to 3%
   (Cologne when labeled as a single word is usually reserved for men's fragrances)

Buy a fragrance with the greatest amount of essential/fragrance oils in it not alcohol. The greater amount of essential/fragrance oil is the best value. There is sometimes confusion at the fragrance counter about this hierarchy but the fragrance categories breakdown listed should help.

Ladies, don't rule out smelling the men's fragrances for yourself. Many women have come to me and said they found men's lines more to their liking especially ladies who are not happy with florals. Also, many women are burning candles, incense sticks and wearing oils which tend to use heavier scents typically found in many male fragrances and because you now like those scents you also like to wear them. Percentages can very somewhat because there is no uniform code but the fragrance. I've included categories that are commonly used.

As a guy, I knew whatever fragrance I put on at home was the only time I would put on a fragrance so it would have to last. When I developed my fragrance the first versions of the scent were light and didn't last long. I used the formula percentage for a cologne. I knew I had to make it stronger to last. I ended up boosting my percentage to 20% a range for a perfume. I didn't categorize my fragrance as a perfume because the majority of men won't wear a perfume and most women wouldn't purchase a perfume for men. Even though in the beginning of fragrances in Europe both men and women wore perfume. Later, gender was marketed and men‘s fragrances were labeled cologne and later aftershaves and unisex.

So my fragrance RAKS was still labeled a cologne for men but my formula was at perfume strength.

It's important for you to stay involved with your fragrance until the end. Make sure it performs they way you want it too. For me, having a cologne for men I would wear it to test its performance. If your doing a fragrance for the opposite gender make sure you let some people in this case for a ladies product like a perfume enough time to give you some good feedback. The most popular label for women in the States is the eau de parfum where in Europe women still wear more perfume.

Smell Vocabulary

It's important for you to use the language of the fragrance industry when describing the scents you smell. Contrasts are either or, it's light or heavy it can't be both at the same time. Stand alones are just that there isn't an opposite to powdery it is or it isn't. A scent can have as many of these descriptions as you like. It's up to you. A scent can be light, sweet, soft and powdery for example.

Using this vocabulary could also be useful when describing your fragrance to the people working with you in developing your fragrance as well as when your fragrance is done and you're describing it to your customers in person or in print advertising.

Contrasts	**Stand -Alone**
Light – Heavy	Powdery
Sweet – Dry	Pungent
Fresh – Stale	Bitter
Warm – Cool	Sharp
Soft – Hard	
Smooth – Harsh	

Fragrance Components (Ingredients)

Fragrances are made up of essential/fragrance oil's, alcohol and water.

Essential/Fragrance Oil – We talked about these in detail before.

Alcohol - What the business uses is special denatured alcohol. Special denatured alcohol which you will see on ingredients labels on fragrance packaging as sda-39c, sda-40a or sda- 40b, these are grades of alcohol. Of these, sda-39c is considered the perfumer's alcohol and it's the one I prefer as well. Denatured meaning taking the "rum out of it". This means you can't drink it (you will get sick). In most states you can only buy small quantities of denatured alcohol without a license. It's like having a liquor store where you must have a special liquor license to sell alcohol based products. One option is to use a high proof vodka (i.e. 90 proof etc...) but stay away from quality brands (they are best used for their initial purpose – smile). Using vodka as an option is just for your personal experiments. When you are ready to market your fragrance line you should use one of the sda grades preferably sda-39c.

Water – You need to use distilled water because it has the least contaminants in each that could affect your formula. We use water to cut down of the alcohol smell that comes from using alcohol. If you use a sda alcohol you don't need to add water because water is already in the sda alcohol.

Alcohol-free - If you want to create an "alcohol free" formula replace the alcohol and water or sda alcohol with either a jojoba oil or grape seed oil. You will have to experiment with these oils to determine which one you prefer. I prefer jojoba oil but that's just me.

A Well Balanced Fragrance

The goal is for you to create a scent that burns off in a uniformed way or what we call well balanced. A well balanced fragrance has at least one top note, one middle note and one base note. All essential/fragrance oils can be categorized by being of one of these notes. The lightest notes as top notes, the next heavier ones are called middle notes and the heaviest notes are base notes.

When you smell a fragrance the first scents you smell are the top notes then the middle notes reveal themselves then the base notes reveal themselves. At stores and in testing we use blotter cards to smell which I also recommend but at some point you need to smell this "burn off" on your skin. Paper can not duplicate your skin and you need to experience the smell as it burns off your skin before giving your okay to the scent or even when you're at the store testing new fragrances for purchase.

We use a pyramid to show this structure and the following pages give you some key points. The current "fragrance pyramid" that demonstrates the process of the burning off of a fragrance using top note, middle note and base notes as labels is credited to Chief chemist William Poucher as the inventor of this concept. Since the 1920's William's pyramid represents the evaporation rates of fragrance ingredients. He used a scale of 100 assigning the oils that evaporated the fastest the lower the numbers. For example, top notes were assigned 1 to 14, middle notes 15 to 60 and base notes 61 to 100.

When you write up a formula for your fragrance fill in the scents you're using to ensure you have a well balanced fragrance. Remember to have at least one scent in each section. Get into the habit of drawing your pyramid formulas.

Also, it's important to write your formulas using the full words "top notes" or "t/n", "middle notes" or "m/n" and "base notes" or "t/n". Don't get sloppy and use "t", "m" and "b" as shorthand.

Remember, the people in the fragrance industry will take note of you using the proper fragrance labeling.

Well Balanced Fragrances

Fragrance Pyramid

Top note (t/n) burns off first.

Middle note (m/n) burns off second.

Base note (b/n) burns off last.

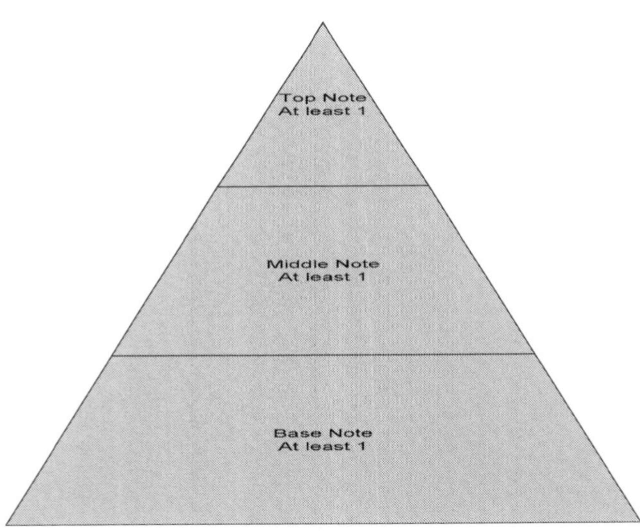

Base Notes (Bottom Notes/ Dry Down)

Oldest of all fragrance ingredients base notes are combined to form chords – a "chord" consists of 2 to 5 base notes mixed together.

Fixative – essential oils known to prolong the life of a scent. ex. frankincense, musk

Woody- sandalwood
Resinous- frankincense
Animal- musk
Balsamic – Peru balsum
Earthy - patchouli
Green - tarragon
Edible – vanilla

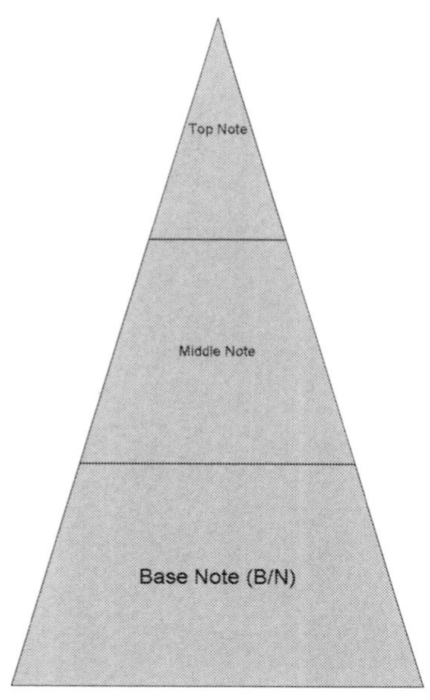

Middle Notes (Heart Notes)

Almost all floral essences are middle notes and the majority of middle notes are florals.

Light- neroli
Spicy – clove
Green –lavender
Rosy- rose
Narcotic - jasmine
Fruity - chamomile
Precious – orange flower

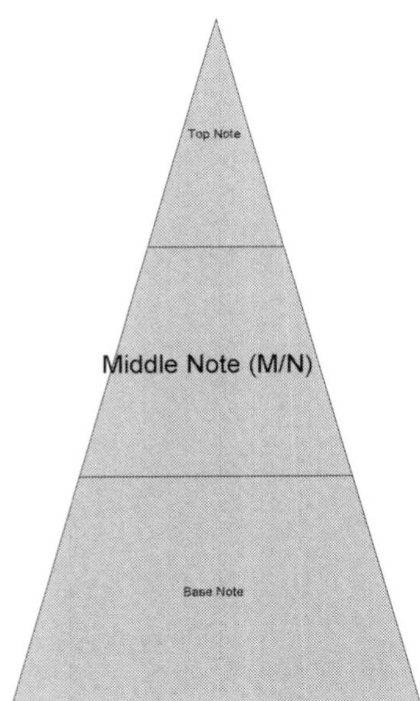

Top Notes (Head Notes)

familiar, uncomplicated

Role of top note – to give the fragrance a starting point.

Citrus – grapefruit

Green-spearmint

Spicy - pepper

Flowery - lavender

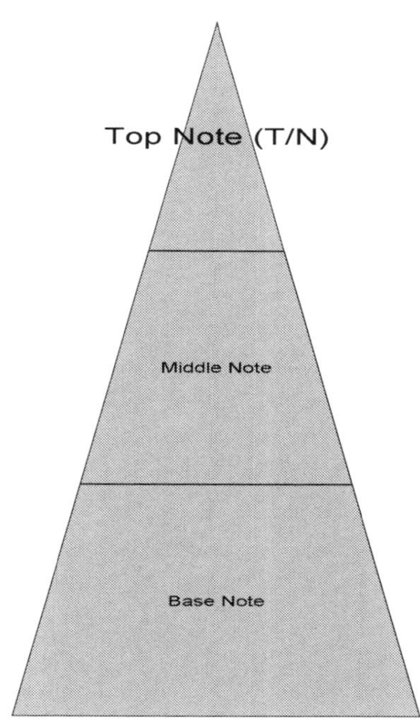

RÄKS

The following are key ingredients of my formula for RAKS cologne for men that I introduced to Nordstrom in 1995 (can't give you my whole formula – it's a secret – Smile).

T/N – maltese orange, Italian bergamot, lavender
M/N – white jasmin, damask rose, cinnamon, clove buds
B/N – sandalwood, patchouli, cedarwood, white musk, vanilla

It took me about 18 months to get the formula for RAKS that I was happy with. I mention this to remind you not to rush; you'll know the smell when you smell it. It has been said that "patience is a virtue."

The Senses

Of our 5 senses (touch, taste, smell, hearing, sight) smell is considered the most powerful because it is the one sense that goes directly to the brain.

All other senses are redirected to an organ called the thalamus before finally arriving at the brain. So this is why when you smell certain things it takes you right back to the last time you smelled that scent, like on a former boyfriend or girlfriend who was a loser! That is why you won't buy it again for someone you do like. Or it can remind you of being a little girl or boy in your mom's kitchen and she just baked you some cookies and you can smell them as if it were yesterday.

Even though the sense of smell is our strongest, it does however have a weakness. Your sense of smell fatigues quickly. You should only smell at most 3 scents before letting your nose take a break. Smelling more than 3 scents in a row causes your sense of smell to go into what the medical community calls "olfactory fatigue." This is when you can't smell any new scents until your nose gets a chance to "reset." Three of the ways to "reset" your sense of smell are (1) getting a breath of fresh air or (2) breathing into a piece of wool cloth or (3) smell some whole coffee beans. I prefer using the coffee beans.

Your Smell Kit

What I recommend when putting your kit together is to use fragrance oils (synthetics) as opposed to essential oils (naturals) because synthetics are less expensive. Also, purchase the smallest sizes possible so you can get the greatest variety of oils. Remember, the greater the variety of oils you can smell the greater your options to use and be familiar with. There might be a scent or scents you never smelled before that you actually might like and want to try.

Also, make sure you buy oils that you might not like because they may surprise you when blending them with other oils. How do I know this? When I first started buying oils, I only bought the ones I liked to smell and when I blended them they didn't blend well. I guess it's like spices, salt works great with pepper. Smell is about balance if something is too sweet you mix it with something bitter to balance it out. Be open to try all different combinations. Write down what you do so if there is a combination you do like you have the formula for it. Two drops of orange and one drop of lemon smells different than two drops of lemon and one drop of orange.

Fun ways to use your kit

Try just sitting down and smelling your favorites, it will relax you. Also, the process of smelling scents might inspire new ideas.

Smell Exercise

Take a piece of paper and create a chart to keep your smell experiments. This will be your source document that you can refer to about what scents you like and why. Never throw away any of your charts keep them in a safe place, make sure you date them. This way you can refer back to your notes before starting to play with different combinations to smell. The "What comes to Mind" column should be what ever you think, don't sensor your self even if you use bad words. The last column you should use the "Smell Vocabulary". As you smell more, you will naturally use more of the vocabulary to describe a single smell.

Essential oil/ Fragrance oil	What comes to Mind	Smell Vocabulary
Coconut	cupcakes, candy	sweet, light, cool
Honeysuckle	shampoo	soft, light
Sandalwood	incense	heavy, warm
French Vanilla	coffee, muffins	soft, light, warm
Cucumber	candy, hair conditioner	sweet, soft
Jasmine	parks, ladies perfume	light, powdery

My Original Smell Kit

Below are the contents of my original scent kit. All my oils were synthetic. I used my budget to get as much of a variety as possible. Why do you hear from people that fragrances all smell alike, its because they are using the same scents other fragrance companies are using, break the mold and add some new scents to the mix. When I started they were 1,200 oils that were available for use in the U.S. fragrance industry to date there are more than 2,000 that are available.

Orange (t/n)

Apricot (t/n)

Lemon (t/n)

Grapefruit (t/n)

Clove (b/n)

Coconut (t/n)

Tangerine (t/n)

Orris Root (b/n)

Lotus (m/n)

Rose (m/n)

Nutmeg (m/n)

Myrrh (b/n)

Strawberry (t/n)

Jasmine (m/n)

Pennyroyal (m/n)

Cinnamon (b/n)

Vanilla (b/n)

Patchouli (b/n)

Sandalwood (b/n)

Frankincense (b/n)

Safety
Rules for all experiments

Wear effective eye protection like protective glasses.

Never attempt to taste any oils they are not for human consumption.

Avoid skin contact of essential oils/fragrance oils. In there present state they are highly concentrated and not intended to be placed on the skin unless you have cut them with alcohol or oils like jojoba or grape seed oil to the appropriate strength.

If you do get oils on your skin make sure to use warm water and soap to clean yourself after you finish using them.

Be careful to smell lightly at first, your nose is not accustomed to highly concentrated oils. Use your hand to “fan” the smell, never “snort” a smell.

Use latex gloves as a way to avoid skin contact.

Never smoke or be around naked flames.

How to do a well balanced fragrance exercise

You will need oils from the following categories: top notes, middle notes and base notes, coffee beans, blotter paper/ paper towel and a pen.

Use the fragrance oils (synthetics) from your kit. Be open to try all different combinations you might be surprised in what turns out. Remember, each time you create a new combination, write down what you did. Two drops of jasmine and one drop of rose is different from two drops of rose and one drop of jasmine.

Coffee beans: buy a bag of coffee beans and use them to "reset" your nose when smelling different oils. Even though our sense of smell is strong you can only smell at most 3 smells before you need to reset your nose. This is every time you smell. I prefer a Columbian whole bean specifically I use Don Francisco's Family Reserve whole bean medium roast. Now remember these are beans for smelling so don't later use these for coffee consumption. If you borrow these beans from your parents or loved one don't put them back in the bag after you smelled on them! Keep them in another container and store with your fragrance oils. I put my coffee beans in a plastic cup or small bowl when I'm smelling. After you have smelled for the day put them back in the coffee bag and seal them before your next use.

The Blotter Card

Having one drop for each note gives you a well balanced fragrance. If you happen to drop more than one drop, don't start over see what happens after you finish you might like it. Sometimes our greatest results come from mistakes. Be sure to write down the oils you use and the number of drops you use. It doesn't matter which oil you start with, just make sure they are on top of each other. Fan your card or breathe on it to accelerate blending but have patience it will take a few minutes for your formula to completely blend together.

Blotter paper is a card stock that is absorbent. If you can get them in 8 ½ by 11 that's okay but cut them in half or in ¼ to maximize use.

If you can't get blotter paper a coffee filter could be used. Coffee filter paper usually comes in round pieces; you can cut them so that you have a square.

Give your card a name or a concept or a category. Who do you thinks it for, a man a women or a child? Maybe it smells like a candle or a room freshener instead. Write down the scents you used and the actual number of drops you used.

Blotter Card

Name: Andre' Barnwell
Category: For Women

Place Drops

Here

	# of Drops
Top Note(s)	
Peach	1
Middle Note(s)	
Gardenia	1
Base Note(s)	
Cedarwood	1

The Paper Towel

If you can't get blotter paper, you can use a paper towel. The paper towels that are prefolded into thirds work the best. If not, take a paper towel and make your folds so that it is in three sections.

Tear the folded paper towel along the folds then label each one t/n, m/n, b/n

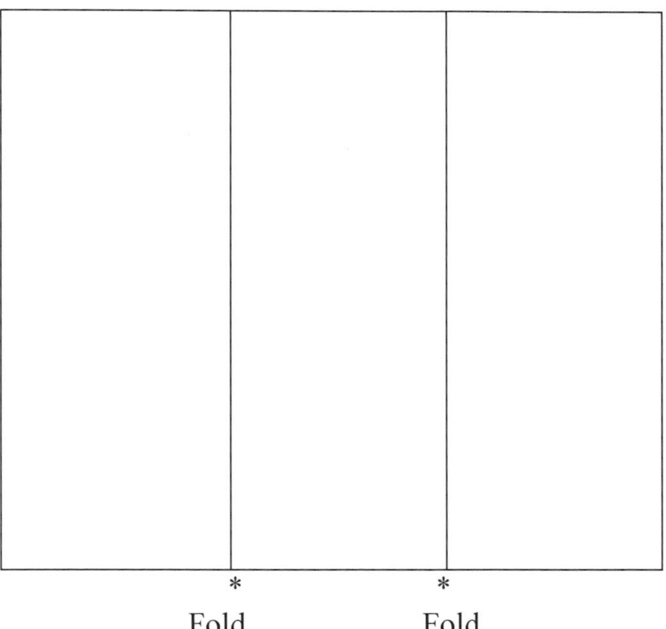

Then label each note with the essential/fragrance oil that you are using.

X – Place for your oil drop.

T/N Peach	M/N Gardenia	B/N Cedarwood
X	X	X

Now put one paper towel section on top of another so that the oil stains overlap. It doesn't matter which order you put them in as long as there are overlapping. Smash the oil stains together so that they blend. Breathe on it to accelerate the blending. Try to use your thumb and index finger only to reduce the amount of oils that get on your hands. You could also use playtex gloves. It will take a few minutes for the oils to blend. Continue to breath and rub on them to accelerate the process. Congratulations, you have created your first well balanced fragrance!

Again if you happened to add more than one drop to any sheets make a note of it first before starting over. As you get better at this feel free to use multiple oils to any note section but make sure you write them done before you drop oil onto your sheets. After your done do not rub your experiments on your skin these oils are highly concentrated and are not designed to go directly on your skin unless they are diluted. After your done make sure you use soap and warm water to wash the oils off your hands.

Music & Fragrance

In 1867, George William Septmus Piesse published the book The Art of Perfumery where he created the odophone scale. This was a musical scale that placed the different smells of aromatherapy oils and assigned them to music notes. Septimus Piesse tried to directly correlate music and scent by assigning scents to music notes. C=Jasmine, D=Vanilla, B=Peppermint etc. As a perfumer himself his idea of creating a great fragrance was like creating a great symphony. You will notice that the fragrance business has adopted key terms from music to describe the art of fragrance. Notes and chords are two terms heavily used in our business.

This way of organizing the blending process did not work because there are many more scents then they are musical notes but appreciation for the way we create musically has some of the same attributes to express what we feel in creating the "perfect" fragrance.

I use music in creation not as literally as Septimus tried to but using music and the sense of hearing to help me express my sense of smell. The type of music I listen to helps me create certain blends. For me, music without lyrics really allows me to get the feel of music or music in another language other than English allows me to hear it without interpreting it. Jazz is one my favorite art forms to get me in the creative "mood." Greats like Miles Davis, Charlie Parker, Thelonious Monk or Tito Puente, their melodic notes tells a story for me.

I also find original music soundtracks to films also put me in that place and again the ones that didn't use lyrics were the most powerful for me.

I have shared this music technique with my students at FIDM and it's a part of their project for my fundamentals of fragrance class. They have to create a well balanced fragrance sampler (it has to have a top note, middle note and base note) for their favorite movie by using the movies original soundtrack. They have to select a music track from the movie that track would take them to a scene in the movie and it's that scene that they have to interpret by giving it a smell.

I am always amazed at their creativity when they give these movies a smell.

So you try it!

1. Pick your favorite movies soundtrack. Listen to all of the tracks until one moves you. That track will take you to a specific scene in the movie. Look at that scene and be inspired by the characters or elements in that scene. Start thinking how to bring that scene to life with at least one top note, one middle note and base note.

2. Cut out a small piece of cardboard where you can fold it like a birthday card. Draw some images of the movie on the front and back. Look at the dvd or cd cover of your movie for ideas. Write the three notes on the inside cover and drop your

oil drops on top of each other on the inside of the back cover in the middle.

You have created your first movie fragrance sampler.

My students have more time in class and would actually use Adobe Photoshop to create a fragrance sample jacket using images from the movie and I supply them a fragrance vial that they fill up with their 3 oils. The specs of the fragrance sampler is 6¼ wide by 4½ tall.

My opinion on music and creating fragrances

Music is such a good medium for creative inspiration and creating an atmosphere for your clients. For me, attending a fashion show is more enjoyable when I feel the designer picked their music wisely. It moves the show.

As a fashion designer, music is an important element for your fashion presentation to create the excitement of your fashion show, launching event or video presentations. Music should also help you transition into the mood of your fragrance ideas. Think of your top notes as your song opening the middle note the bridge and the base notes as your grand finally. Whether you play an instrument, can sing or just listen to music, use it as a way to get into the "mood."

Jazz is my thing but I listen to all types of music as well. Any music will work if it inspires you. In the end, we are all different yet the same.

For me, "Fragrance creation is like Jazz, it's about bending the notes." From time to time I still pick up my soprano sax and play for inspiration.

FRAGRANCE SAMPLES

The fragrance industry is not good at making samples available other than at the time of launching a new line and I think that's unfortunate. It cost me 23 cents to make a sample and I was asking 42 dollars for my fragrance. I always thought that was a good deal for the potential purchase. I would insist that your line has samples as well and not just during the launch.

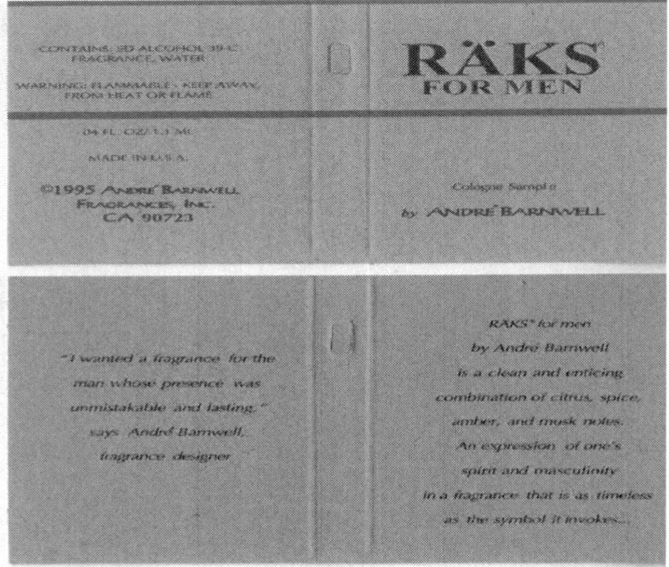

I can't over emphasis the importance of fragrance samples and what they can do for you. In my own experience, I was going home for the holidays from California to Pennsylvania. There was a big storm and my flight was cancelled. The airline did get me on another flight but it connected in Ohio. The one thing you want to avoid in flying back east in the winter time is connecting especially in northern cities where you might get stuck there. Well, I could have gotten upset but I thought I'm going home for the holidays and nothing was going to dampen my spirit. When I boarded this new flight it was packed and I was sitting in the emergency row next to one person.

I keep a portfolio case with me where I have some fragrance samples and pictures of my product and notes on any ideas for the line I'm working on. About 30 minutes into the flight to Ohio, I noticed the guy next to me was an actor and he was reading a film script. I opened my portfolio and was thinking of ways to expand my line from the two Los Angeles boutiques stores that my fragrance was in. Shortly there after the guy asked me what I did just to start conversation. He probably was tired of reading the script and was taking a break. My first thought was that I didn't feel like talking but I reminded myself that I was going home and I should maintain a cheerful sprit. So I told him I was a fragrance designer and he inquired a bit more so I told him my story. I gave him a sample from my portfolio he thanked me and went back to reading his script. Five minutes later he asked me if I had another sample he enjoyed the smell and that his girlfriend was a Nordstrom fragrance buyer in LA and that she would be seeing him over the holidays in Ohio and he would give it to her (I liked the fact that he didn't want to give her his sample). He couldn't promise me a response from her but he would definitely give it to her and tell her what he thought of it. I thanked him for his offer and wished him a happy holiday. I went home didn't mention the encounter to my family because I didn't want to get my hopes up.

When I got back to LA I did get a call from his girlfriend in late January and my fragrance was in the Nordstrom Store South Bay by February. I truly believe this was meant to happen but what if I didn't have those samples with me. I never went anywhere without samples with me because you never know what could happen!

Testing fragrances at a Retail Counter

Allow the fragrance to breath on your skin. Let it sit on your skin a few minutes (2 to 4 minutes) so that you experience the various levels of smell.

If your testing more than one fragrance make sure you use different places on your arm so that the fragrances don't overlap. If they overlap and you like the smell you'll have to buy both fragrances to recreate that scent. Also remember which one is which. I would try no more than three at a time to reduce confusion. If there are some other fragrances that interest you ask for a sample to try later.

Most people buy fragrances based on the top note but the base note is what their scent is going to smell like for the longest period of time. While your in the store with the scent on, do some other browsing or shopping you planned for the next five to ten minutes and come back to the counter when the scent kicks in, if you like it at this point buy it or if your lucky whoever is with you buys it for you as a gift!

How to apply a scent

A couple things you should know about your skin and how these factors affect how fragrances react on you.

If you have dry skin, think of your skin as a frying pan with no oil in it when fragrance is applied to your skin it burns off quickly. So you will need an oil on your skin first. After taking a warm bath or shower apply a very light coating of petroleum jelly on your skin or unscented body oil. The jelly/oil will hold the scent on your body longer. Because the jelly/oil is unscented it doesn't add any unwanted combination of smells to your favorite scents.

Oily skin? Yes, your pan is already oiled so when you apply scent it burns off the oil on your skin first then the scent. In your case the scent will last longer on oily skin.

Combination skin – you need to do a combination of what you would do for dry skin and what you would do for oily skin. As a general rule, never apply a scent directly to your face. Your face is too sensitive for this application and should never be done. Pulse points like behind the ear is only exception. Scent yourself from the neck down. Interestingly enough you should start at your ankles and work your way up. Scent rises so the lower you apply the longer it will last as an experience on your body.

So which products should you have in your line? First, you should have samples, samples, samples! Start with a 1.7oz spray, later when your customers are enjoying your fragrance introduce a 3.4 oz spray. If you can afford a perfume go for it, it is the best value but American women especially younger ones are conditioned to buy the sprays. European women are the biggest buyers of perfume. If you choose a spray go with the highest concentration, Eau de Parfum.

Next a cream, moisturizer or lotion? Creams will hold your fragrance the best. They are the richest in ingredients and subsequently are the most expensive. Then comes a moisturizer, not as many ingredients as the cream so is the next less expensive to produce and the lotion in the least expensive. I suggest a cream or moisturizer if you can afford it, your customers will notice the quality difference. Also with so many other fragrances on the market that have a lotion, your brand will stand out even further.

I'm not a big fan of cleaning products or deodorants with scents in them. I think your customers should use those products that they are already using. I believe our role is to provide a scent experience where your customers can still use the products that work best on their skin to clean or deodorize the body.

Now this combination of products might alter the way the fragrance smells on you because of the scents in the other products but this will also allow the scent to smell a little different on you as opposed to someone else wearing the same fragrance.

Body gels/washes are a good addition to a line as long as they are not too strong. Remember they are designed to clean your skin. Because they are scented and you could expose them to sensitive areas of your body be very careful in using them.

I mentioned pulse points before and why are they important? Pulse points are located wherever your heartbeat is closest to the skin surface. Behind the ears, nape of neck, bosom, crook of elbows, wrists, behind the knees and ankles. The heat that is generated from these areas assists in the release of your fragrance.

Remember when you are applying a fragrance start at the bottom and work your way up. Start with you ankles, behind your knees, inside elbow, bosom and behind the ears. Fragrance rises when it heats up from your body temperature it will rise up thru your clothes thus lasting longer.

Most importantly, I would never use them on my head or face (except for behind the ears). Our faces and heads are very sensitive I would continue to use the face products I'm already using for the head and face. They are called body products for a reason!

Fragrance Wardrobing

When you purchase fragrances with additional products in the line they are intended to help in your smelling pleasure. We call this fragrance layering or what the beauty industry calls fragrance wardrobing.

Fragrance wardrobing works best when your fragrance is very light and it's hard to maintain a scent for long periods. For those of you who enjoy floral scents this is especially true. Have your floral fragrance with a shower gel, lotion and or cream. This technique will allow the scent to last longer on your body.

The other fragrance families are stronger by definition and layering might be too much scent for you. I recommend with strong fragrances go with an unscented cream or moisturizer as well as body gel so that when you do apply your fragrance you have the one uniformed scent you were after. Remember everything you put on that has a scent will interact with your fragrance and that interaction will be the smell you walk around with.

Alternate Fragrances

If you don't want to create a personal care fragrance consider the following alternatives:

Environmental fragrance – scents/aromas that are added to your surroundings like incense. Sticks or cones are very popular in this category.

Home fragrance – scents designed specifically for use in home like a scented candle. They are made from both natural and synthetic materials both safe and of high quality ingredients that are also found in fragrances.

You could also use these fragrance alternatives as line extensions to your fragrance. I started with RAKS as a 1.7 oz spray then I added a 3.4 oz size, then a body shampoo and then a body moisturizer. I finally included RAKS incense which I gave away as a gift with purchase. What I found out later was my female customers were giving the fragrance to their boyfriends/husbands and keeping the incense for themselves. How cool!

Often Asked Questions

Do fragrances smell different on different people?

Yes. They are so many variables that could change a smell on each of us. Our individual chemistry, our genes, skin type, hair colors, the diet all contribute. Imagine if you enjoy spicy foods like garlic. Garlic will be released thru the skin. Meat eaters smell differently from vegans.

Will growing older effect our sense of smell?

Yes. As we grow older we slowly lose our sense of smell. When this starts to happen continue to put on the same amount of scent you always have even though you might think it's strong enough.

How long will a fragrance last?

Fragrance should last about 4 hours if blended correctly. Lighter scents will need to be applied more frequently.

How does your skin type factor in on how long a fragrance will last?

Oily skin holds fragrance longer than combination or dry skin. If you have dry skin you need to apply a moisturizer to mimic the oily skin if you want your fragrances to last longer on your skin. But remember all skin is sensitive and be careful not to irritate your skin.

How do you store a fragrance?

Once you open the bottle the evaporation process begins and never really stops. Yes, putting you fragrance in cool area out of and direct sunlight will slow down the process. Some people put their fragrance in the refrigerator and that will slow down the evaporation process as well. But my suggestion is to enjoy you fragrances, buy different ones to change it up and when it's empty buy another one.

Do people wear fragrance according the seasons?

Yes. Normally during colder winter months you would were a heavier scent and in warmer months you would wear lighter fragrances like fruits, citruses and florals. But at the end of the day wear what makes you feel good regardless of the weather.

Business Planning Process Fragrance Brief

"The Discussion"

You are getting exposure and success with your fashion line. One of the people you meet is interested in talking to you about a fragrance line. First, never sign ANYTHING without the approval of a lawyer that is representing your interests.

You are having your first meeting what should you cover. Sometimes this is called the fragrance brief, points that should be a part of the items you want to cover that would eventually become elements of a subsequent contract.

The Brief should consist of confidentiality, the product(s), target market, the fragrance marketing plan and the fragrance follow up.

<u>Confidentiality</u> – the conversation you are having should be confidential to the parties in the room, your ideas are valuable and should be considered as such.

<u>Product(s)</u> – what do you want to create? I started with a 1.7 oz spray only with samples and when my customers' sales increase I then introduced the 3.4 oz spray and later other products like a body shampoo, body lotion and incense stick. Start small and grow is always a good strategy.

Target Market – be clear as to who your target audience is. Is that the same group that supports your clothing line, think demographics, psychographics, behavioral and geographic considerations? Or are you looking to expose your brand beyond your original target market. For example, say your clothing line is very expensive and you can use your fragrance as an affordable product in your product line.

Marketing Plan – how do you see the product being launched? What type of strategies are they thinking about, advertising, media strategy including social media, word of mouth etc.?

Follow-up - this is how they are going to develop the product usually 3 things to do to test the product itself. How do they evaluate the technical performance of the scent usually done inside of the lab, a limited panel test outside the lab to key people and a full panel test i.e. a customer panel to get real feedback about the smell. Before you agree with any scent, you should have a full panel test so that you have a good indication what your target market's reaction to your scent is going to be.

Your Fragrance

More than likely two scenarios will probably present themselves.

Your investor of your fashion line might increase their commitment to you to finance a fragrance line or a license opportunity will present itself. Most fashion designers go with licensing; it's pretty common in the business. My piece of advice is to still hire someone with a fragrance background that you trust to oversee the project for you.

House of Representatives

H. R. No. 1385
By: Representative Jones of the 71st

A RESOLUTION

Recognizing Andre Barnwell; and for other purposes.

WHEREAS, seven years ago, entrepreneur fragrance designer Andre Barnwell had no samples, no sports star endorsement, not even a business card, but he had a dream, a penchant for hard work, and a fragrance he believed would be embraced by men seeking a modern classic cologne, a product he called Raks (pronounced "Rocks"); and

WHEREAS, Andre and his brother, Harold, were raised by their army sergeant major father and school teacher mother to believe in their own potential and always to rely on family, so the two were natural partners in the fledgling fragrance business which Andre envisioned, and so when they were unable to attract investment capital, they raised the start-up money themselves and began selling their cologne on a small scale; and

WHEREAS, finally, fate stepped in and lent a hand when Andre found himself on an airplane sitting next to the boyfriend of a buyer for Nordstrom, and a casual contact was the catalyst that converted preparation and hard work into success, and now Raks is sold in numerous locations and is competing quite well against products backed by deep pockets and endorsed by super stars; and

WHEREAS, it is only fitting that this body recognize the work and perseverence exhibited by Andre Barnwell.

NOW, THEREFORE, BE IT RESOLVED BY THE HOUSE OF REPRESENTATIVES that the members of this body commend Andre Barnwell for his success and wish him every success in the future.

BE IT FURTHER RESOLVED that the Clerk of the House of Representatives is authorized and directed to transmit an appropriate copy of this resolution to Andre Barnwell.

IN HOUSE
Read and Adopted
March 19, 1998

Robert E. Rivers, Jr.
Clerk

Thanks to my brother Harold, Representative Jones and my customers who shopped at the Nordstrom's in Atlanta, Ga. Their belief in me made this resolution a reality.

Your fragrance is not just liquid in a bottle; it is your brand mantra in a bottle or what we call the heart and soul of your brand in a bottle.

When a customer applies your fragrance to their skin they are literally "wearing" your brand. A woman, who is wearing J'adore Dior parfum, is having the same emotional experience as if she were wearing a Dior dress. This relationship between your clothing line, fragrance and how customers view it is why a fragrance has and continues to be the perfect brand category extension to your clothing line.

"What do I wear in bed? Why, Chanel NO.5, of course."

– Marilyn Monroe

Good luck
Fashion Designers!!!!

Bibliography and suggested readings

Morris, T. Edwin, Scents of Time, Perfume from Ancient Egypt to the 21st Century, Bulfinch Press, 1999.

Purvis, Debbie, The Business of Beauty: Cosmetic Retailing, Wall & Emerson, Inc., 1994.

Ackerman, Diane, A Natural History of Senses, Random House, 1990.

Pavia, Fabienne, The World of Perfume, Knicker Bocker Press, 1995.

Ginsberg, Steve, Reeking Havoc, Hutchinson Business Books, 1989.

Moran, Jan, Fabulous Fragrances, Crescent House Publishing, 1994.

Curtis, Tony and Williams, David, Introduction to Perfumery, Micelle Press, 2nd Edition, 2001.

Booth, Nancy, Perfumes, Splashes & Colognes, Storey Publishing, 1997.

"Perfume: The Essence of Illusion" National Geographic, October 1998, 94-119.

Notes

Notes

Notes

Notes

Made in the USA
San Bernardino, CA
03 June 2017